I Can Write Instructions

Anita Ganeri

D1077089

www.raintreepublishers.co.uk
Visit our website to find out
more information about
Raintree books.

To order:
☎ Phone 0845 6044371
🖷 Fax +44 (0) 1865 312263
🖳 Email myorders@raintreepublishers.co.uk

Customers from outside the UK please telephone +44 1865 312262

Raintree is an imprint of Capstone Global Library Limited,
a company incorporated in England and Wales having its
registered office at 7 Pilgrim Street, London, EC4V 6LB
– Registered company number: 6695582

Text © Capstone Global Library Limited 2013
First published in hardback in 2013
First published in paperback in 2013
The moral rights of the proprietor have been asserted.

Edited by Daniel Nunn, Rebecca Rissman, and Sian Smith
Designed by Victoria Allen
Picture research by Elizabeth Alexander
Original illustrations © Capstone Global Library Ltd 2013
Illustrated by Victoria Allen and Darren Lingard
Production by Victoria Fitzgerald
Originated by Capstone Global Library Ltd
Printed and bound in China by Leo Paper Products Ltd

ISBN 978 1 406 23831 0 (hardback)
16 15 14 13 12
10 9 8 7 6 5 4 3 2 1

ISBN 978 1 406 23838 9 (paperback)
17 16 15 14 13
10 9 8 7 6 5 4 3 2 1

British Library Cataloguing in Publication Data
Ganeri, Anita, 1961-
    Instructions. -- (I can write)
    1. Written communication--Juvenile literature.
    I. Title II. Series
    808'.066-dc23

Acknowledgements
We would like to thank the following for permission to reproduce
photographs and artworks: Alamy p.7 (© Nick Gregory);
iStockphoto pp.12 (© Scott Griessel), 14 (© ac_bnphotos);
Shutterstock pp.4 (© AISPIX), 5 (© Milos Luzanin), 8 (© Gelpi), 9
(© Golden Pixels LLC), 10 (© Noam Armonn), 13 (© OtnaYdur), 15
(© DVARG), (19 (© spaxiax), 20 (© BW Folsom), 21 (© Madlen),
21 (© Nataliia Natykach), 22 (© Terrie L. Zeller), 23 (© wacpan),
23 (© Nayuco), 24 (© Fotokostic), 25 (© Oleksii Sagitov), 26
(© Somjade Boonyarat), 27 (© Igor Dutina); Superstock p.6
(© Onoky).

Every effort has been made to contact copyright holders
of material reproduced in this book. Any omissions will
be rectified in subsequent printings if notice is given to the
publisher.

Contents

Some words are shown in bold, **like this**. You can find out what they mean in the glossary on page 30.

What is writing?

When you put words on paper or on a computer screen, you are writing. Learning to write clearly is important so that your readers can understand what you mean.

What do you like writing about?

These instructions tell you how to wash a piece of clothing.

There are many different types of writing. This book is about instructions. Instructions are a type of **non-fiction**. This means that they are about facts.

What are instructions?

Instructions are **step-by-step** guides that explain how to do or make something. This might be something such as baking a cake or playing a game.

You follow instructions when you are cooking.

Some instructions can be difficult to follow.

Instructions need to be clear and simple so that the reader can follow them. Before you start writing, think about what needs to be done, and in which order.

Different instructions

There are lots of different types of instructions. If you want to learn how to play a musical instrument, you need to follow some instructions.

You need instructions to learn how to play the guitar.

Instructions help you learn to look after a pet.

You might also be given instructions on how to stay safe, find your way, or make models. A vet might give you instructions for looking after a new pet.

Good instructions

When you are writing instructions, think about the title. It should tell the reader what he or she is going to make or do. Instructions should be short and snappy.

How to brush your teeth

This title tells the reader the aim of the instructions.

Think about what you need to say in your instructions. Make sure that they are in the right order. Use short, clear **sentences** so that your reader does not get muddled.

Here are some things to include when you are writing instructions.

Things to include

- **title**
- **list of equipment needed**
- **list of steps**
- **diagram**

Writing style

Use bossy **verbs** to write your instructions. These give orders and tell readers what to do. They make your instructions easier to understand.

Here are some bossy verbs. Can you think of any more?

Bossy verbs

jump

cut

stir

draw

fold

Write the steps in the correct order. You can use words called **time connectives** to help you. Look at the list of time connectives below.

Can you think of any more time connectives?

first
next
then
after
finally

Making lists

Write down the **equipment**, tools, or **ingredients** that the reader needs. Write this as a list. You can use **bullet points** to make the list clear for your reader.

Making jelly

You will need:

- **jelly powder or cubes**
- **boiling water**
- **a jug**
- **a bowl**
- **a wooden spoon**

> Make sure that you have not forgotten anything.

Make a list of the steps that the reader needs to follow. Make sure that they are in the right order. You can use numbers to make the order clear.

Remember to add any safety warnings to your instructions. For example 'Ask an adult to help with boiling the water.'

1. Put the jelly powder or cubes in the bowl.

2. Pour the water in and stir.

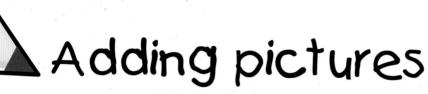

Adding pictures

You can add pictures or **diagrams** to make your instructions clearer. It is useful to number these so that they match the list of steps.

Here you can see some of the steps in making a robot.

Making a model robot

1. **Stick a small box on top of a large box. This is the robot's head.**

2. **Stick on cardboard tubes for its arms and legs.**

1.

If you are telling the reader how to make something, show a picture of the finished item. Add labels to explain what the different parts are.

Draw lines from the labels to the right parts of your diagram.

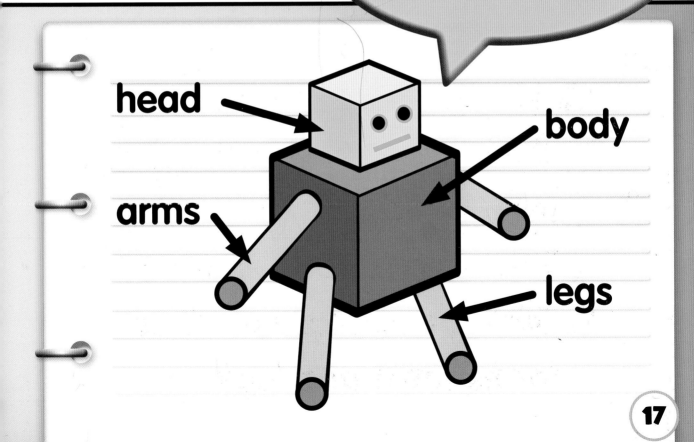

head

body

arms

legs

In the right order

Read the instructions below. They tell you how to wash your hands but they are jumbled up in the wrong order.

These instructions make no sense.

Put soap on your hands.

Dry your hands on the towel.

Rinse the soap off.

Turn on the tap.

Rub your hands together.

Turn off the tap.

Wet your hands.

Can you sort the instructions out and put them in the right order? You can number them to make the order clear.

> Add numbers to the instructions.

1. **Turn on the tap.**

2. **Wet your hands.**

3. **Put soap on your hands.**

4. **Rub your hands together.**

5. **Rinse the soap off.**

6. **Turn off the tap.**

7. **Dry your hands on the towel.**

Making a sandwich

Try writing some instructions for making a jam sandwich. Start with the title and a list of things that the reader will need.

Use **bullet points** for your list.

Make a sandwich

You will need:

- **bread**
- **butter**
- **jam**
- **knife**
- **plate**

Write down your **step-by-step** instructions. Make sure that they are in the right order. Here is the first one to start you off.

Can you write the rest of the steps?

1. Put two slices of bread on the plate.

2. ???

3. ???

Making a birthday card

Making a birthday card is fun. Can you write some instructions for making a card? Keep them simple and easy to follow.

Find out if your instructions work by asking someone to try them out.

It can help if you make your own card first. Then you can write down the steps you used to make it. Here are some 'bossy' words to help you.

Can you use these words in your instructions?

Helpful words

fold

cut

draw

stick

colour

 Playing football

Imagine that you are writing to your **penfriend**. He or she has never played football before. Write some instructions to explain how you play football.

How do you tell someone to play football?

Think of all the things that you need to explain. For example, you need to say how many players there are in a team, how long to play for, and how to win a game.

Here are some words to help you.

Helpful words

team

ball

pitch

goal

kick

Growing a sunflower

On these two pages, you can read some instructions for growing a sunflower. Look at the 'You will need' list. Is there anything missing from it?

Grow a sunflower

You will need:

- **a pot**
- **soil**
- **water**

The answer is: a sunflower seed!

Look at the steps below. They are jumbled up. Can you put them in the right order? Can you think of any more steps?

You could add a final step: Water your seed every day.

Push the seed into the soil.

Fill the pot with soil almost to the top.

Water the soil.

Cover the seed with soil.

Top tips for writing instructions

1. Always read your instructions through to make sure that they are in the right order and make sense.

2. Imagine that you are explaining things to an alien from another planet who has never done them before.

3. Look at other instructions, such as those on packets or tins of food, in recipe books, on computer games, and so on. It will help you in your writing.

4. Keep your **sentences** short so that they are easy to understand. If you use difficult words, make sure that you explain them.

5. Add any safety tips to your instructions. For example, if you are telling someone how to make a sandwich, they need to be careful when they are using a knife.

6. Look at a board game or jigsaw puzzle. What do you think of the instructions? Are they simple and clear? Can you follow them easily?

7. Make your writing style friendlier by saying 'You…', or more **formal** by just using bossy words to give orders.

8. Keep practising! Writing is like learning to ride your bike, or roller skating. You need to keep practising.

 Glossary

bullet points small dots that are used instead of numbers in a list

diagram picture showing how something works

equipment the things you might need to make something, for example scissors, glue, and card to make a model

formal language that is correct and follows the rules

ingredients list of the different foods you need to make something, such as a cake

non-fiction writing that is about real people or things

penfriend friend you write to, even though you may never have met him or her

sentence group of words that makes sense on its own

step-by-step explaining something in order, one step after the other

time connective word or words that say when something happened

verb doing, or action, word

Find out more

Books

Getting to Grips with Grammar series, Anita Ganeri (Raintree Publishing, 2012)

Rip the Page! Adventures in Creative Writing, Karen Benke (Trumpeter Books, 2010)

Websites

www.bbc.co.uk/schools/ks1bitesize/literacy

www.bbc.co.uk/schools/ks2bitesize/english/writing

Index